The Battle of Adobe Walls:
A Bit of Frontier History, Told to the Narrator by the Men who Made It

Edward Campbell Little
(1858–1924)

Republished from:
"The Battle of Adobe Walls,"
Edward Campbell Little,
Pearson's Magazine,
January 1908, pp. 75-85

THE Kansas buffalo hunters invaded the Texas Panhandle and the Llano Estacado in force in the spring of 1874; in five months it is said they slew a hundred thousand bison. The deserted Adobe Walls, a station established by Spanish friars, French Canadian hunters or General Howe's soldiers, was selected as the rendezvous for these hunters, who came from Dodge City, one hundred and seventy-five miles away. Three "business houses" and a blacksmith shop gave token of approaching civilization, and about them congregated all the adventurous spirits of the Southwest, far from the protection of any military post, and probably unknown to the slow-moving authorities who wore the badge of red tape.

The threats of an approaching raid might have been heard among the exasperated Indians, who saw their means of subsistence being absolutely destroyed. Quanah, the son of a Texas girl named Parker (captive from her childhood among the Comanches, who in after years preferred her Indian family to her white kinsfolk, whom she revisited), and e then war chief of the Comanches, lost his most intimate friend and companion in some altercation with the buffalo hunters, and soon after this occurrence the old Medicine Man of the tribe was announcing "good medicine" that would enable the braves to slay the white men at Adobe Walls as they slumbered. By the last of June the Indians were ready to begin the campaign in which Nelson A. Miles won a star and Quanah Parker began that supremacy among the Comanches which he still retains. As they galloped leisurely across the grassy bottoms of the Canadian an hour or sa before sunrise, on that memorable June day, the Indians formed a gorgeous and spectacular cavalcade. They rode nine hundred strong, the picked men of the Comanche, Kiowa, Cheyenne and Arapahoe nations, the finest horsemen on earth, the best cavalry that ever went to battle. Yellow with ochre, red with vermilion, stained with every horrible decorative device in the hideous art catalogue of the plains, their ponies shone with all the colors of the red skin rainbow.

Glistening with war paint and decked in his battle raiment, every Indian believed that he galloped to the certain victory the Medicine Man prophesied. Some could boast no gayer apparel than a breech clout, a war whoop and an anxious look. Other tawny shoulders were covered by calico shirts, the owners of which gathered closely about them the almost inevitable faded army blanket. Dyed porcupine quills edged occasional moccasins, and elaborate beadwork designs ornamented many a buckskin shirt. Flannel streamers quivering with feathers fluttered about them. Each carried a quirt at his wrist. Trappings of fur, bracelets of silver and marvelous feathered head-dresses testified to the Comanche love of finery. Buffalo-rib bows, made by binding together with buffalo-hide thongs the ends of two ribs as deftly, as closely and as firmly as a black smith could have welded his metals, proved the existence of Cheyenne mechanical skill. Though they still carried bow, arrow, shield, lance, war club and tomahawk, the Indians had dealt with the traders for more deadly weapons. Forty-five caliber Colt's were frequent, Winchester rifles and Spencer carbines were seen on every side, and sometimes Sharp's rifles.

At their head rode the Comanche, Quanah, and the grim old Medicine Man on a Hide gray pony — destined to prove in his own person the fallacy of his prediction that his medicine made all invulnerable to the white man's bullet. With them, on a bay stallion, came the Comanche sub-chief, Stone Calf's nephew — priest and paladins side by side.

This young chief was armed with pistol and carbine of the latest patterns. His deerskin moccasins were adorned with beads and his leggins were of well-tanned leather. On his right wrist he carried a little square musical instrument four or five inches across, the cadence of which furnished time in dancing. On the cheek strap of his riding bridle was a dark-haired scalp about two inches in diameter, carefully dressed and curiously painted on the inner side. His nine-foot lance, decked with eagle feathers, tipped with a steel point of eighteen inches, was carried with care in a case of otter skin that would have brought him many dollars at the fur trader's. His shield, of two thicknesses of hide from the neck of a buffalo bull, flint dry, capable of turning a pistol ball, and stuffed with feathers, swung from his left arm. This shield was covered with the softest buckskin, the edge hung round with eagle feathers, while on it his coat of arms — a full moon and a group of stars — was emblazoned in ochre. From the shield dangled his medicine, the bill of an eagle, the claws of a bear, and the scalp of a fair-haired man, taken in battle.

More than a foot above his head rose the crest of his splendid war-bonnet, the crowning effort of barbaric art. Covered with lines of beads and artistically wrought with Indian designs, the head-piece was arched with a ridge of handsome eagle feathers. A tail of the very finest buckskin gaily ornamented and trimmed at either edge with eagle feathers, trailed to his heels. A buckskin shirt, fringed with leather laces, covered his coppery breast, and his blanket flowed from his shoulders like the folds of a Roman toga. Straight, supple, and sinewy as an Iroquois was this favorite son of the Comanches.

A mile to their front lay the twenty-eight buffalo hunters at the Adobe Walls, without guard or sentry. They slept in fancied security, or in that careless indifference to danger born of years of peril and excitement. The three buildings of the settlement stood in a row. On the south was the store of Rath & Wright Company, with one of the partners, James Langton, in charge. This building was thirty feet by sixty, had walls of adobe two feet thick, and a big door on the west; in its rear fifteen thousand buffalo hides were arranged in piles. Perhaps one hundred yards, or less, to the north was Hanrahan's adobe building, eighty feet long, twenty-five feet wide and with walls some two feet thick. Some fifty yards to the north of Hanrahan's was the Leonard & Myers store, with Fred Leonard in charge. This structure was thirty feet by seventy-five and its wooden walls were ten inches thick; a big door opened on the east. This store stood in the northeast corner of a stockade two hundred and fifty feet by three hundred, the poles extending seven feet into the ground and from seven to thirteen feet above. There was no chinking between the poles of the stockade or corral. A mess house stood in the southwest corner of the stockade, and between the two buildings was a well.

Tom Keefe's little sod blacksmith shop between Hanrahan's and Leonard's was unoccupied that day, as was Leonard's mess house. The buildings all faced east.

A short quarter of a mile behind were the hills, the rough Breaks of the Canadian. Perhaps two hundred and fifty yards south of Langton's were low sand hills covered with plum bushes. Four hundred yards or more east of Leonard's and Hanrahan's frowned a rugged butte. At its base, heavily fringed with willow, Cottonwood, hackberry and chinaberry trees, ran the little Adobe Walls Creek, now Bent Creek, southeast, toward the approaching enemy and the mile-wide quicksand bed of the Canadian River, a mile and a half away.

Fort Dodge, Dodge City and safety were one hundred and seventy-five miles to the northeast that 27th day of June, 1874. Twelve hundred yards across, carpeted with high blue-stem, curtained by the Breaks of the Canadian, the little valley of Adobe Walls furnished the buffalo hunters an ample, sufficient and glorious amphitheater for their fight against the odds of thirty to one.

Riding easily, without alignment, about twenty-five abreast and deeper, the attacking party swept down on the hunters' camp. Four men and the only white woman in the Southwest slept behind barred floors at Langton's. A few yards away in his blankets on the ground was Tom Keefe, the black smith, and his dog. Thirteen men were sleeping in and about Leonard's, whose big door swung invitingly open.

The Indians were within five or six hundred yards, and in two minutes more theirs would have been good medicine, the buffalo hunters would have been dead, killed with war clubs as they slept. But the chapter of accidents flew open for half a second.

That Texas June morning a rotten cottonwood log upheld the universe for the Kansas hunters; if a sound Cottonwood beam had been set as a ridge-pole in the west end of Hanrahan's place over the bar, not a man would have escaped from Adobe Walls. The crack of a breaking timber aroused every body in Hanrahan's during the night; the dirt roof threatened to fall, and the situation demanded their arduous and extended attention. By considerable labor the men propped up the falling beam, and Hanrahan sent Welch and Shepherd to shovel dirt from the roof to lighten the weight. The first rays of the morning sun were beginning to kindle the prairie, and Billy Dixon was astir at his wagon a few yards away. The young fellows lined up at the bar to take a drink, after their work, and as they were all going hunting that day, they decided to remain up and make an early start. Watson and Ogg went outside for the horses, lariated some five hundred yards to the northeast.

Over near Langton's, Tom Keefe's little dog licked his face and awakened him, to observe a herd of buffalo coming. Keefe lay on his elbow to watch them.

As they walked out in the grass, Watson and Ogg glanced toward the herd, and suddenly from the throat of one of the two came an appalling cry that still rings in the memory of every man who was in Hanrahan's adobe.

The discovered Indians answered with the war whoop — the advancing herd of buffalo was transformed into a pack of yelling, screeching Indian demons. Putting quirts to their ponies, the red phalanx rode straight for Hanrahan's.

Tom Keefe seized his blankets, ran to Langton's and pounded on the door. Jimmy Langton sprang out of bed and admitted him, yet not so quickly but that the Indians fired through the open door as they came on. "They were right on top of us," says Jimmy.

Watson and Ogg hesitated for a moment, then turned and ran fur Hanrahan's adobe. Welch and Shepherd sprang from the roof. Dixon, supposing the Indians were merely after the horses lariated to the northeast, paused for an instant to tie his riding horse to his wagon, but, quickly undeceived, ran to Hanrahan's. The hunters outside fired one volley and retreated within when the Indians were within a hundred yards.

"Save your fire for thirty yards!" yelled Jim Hanrahan, old government wagon-master and experienced frontiersman:

Inside Hanrahan's adobe were ten men, seven armed with buffalo fifty-caliber guns, some of them were best marksmen on the plains. At thirty yards the effect of such a volley from such men was terrific — the formation of the aborigines was split in twain, as it cut by a butcher's cleaver.

"Gents to the right and ladies to the left," called young Shepherd, in pleasant recollection of social functions at Dodge City.

One division swung to the left and swooped down on Langton's, where James Langton, George Ebey, Thomas Keefe, William Olds and one other man gave battle, protecting Mrs. William Olds and a large stock of goods which had come down from Dodge City in nineteen wagons.

To the right, dashed another division, riding straight for Leonard's open door.

A smaller band swung farther to the right to where the horses were picketed.

At the first shots, Fred Leonard, who was in his corral, ran into his store, where fifteen thousand rounds of fixed ammunition and a large stock of goods baited the raiders. As he swung the door to, the foe were only thirty feet away and firing as they came, Quanah in the lead. Old Sam Smith, sans culotte, gun in one hand and cartridge belt in the other, was the last man to enter. As the bar went down the horses of the Indians struck the door till it bent before them, and Adobe Walls was aflame with the fire of the buffalo hunters beginning a three days' fight for their lives.

War Chief Quanah, riding swiftly by Hanrahan's place, saw the open door at Leonard's and rode straight at it, thinking, as he recently said, that they could easily force their way in; but a gun-barrel suddenly appeared through the doorway, and Quanah was shot through the breast and put out of the battle for that day. As he tells of it, he throws a great sprawling hand over his breast, and over his swarthy visage creeps a mingled look of pain and gratitude — pain as he recalls the wound and gratitude for his narrow escape.

His wound was quickly avenged. Around the corner, just north of the stockade, slept Ike and Shorty Shadier in their wagon. Only the night before they had come in from Palo Duro Creek with a load of buffalo hides belonging to Brick Bond, their employer. Farthest from safety, and camped where they could not see the Indians approaching, they were caught, killed and scalped in their wagon — the only men about Adobe Walls who failed to reach a place of safety that morning. Their little dog, which seemed to have endeavored to give them warning, was also scalped. One of the boys had left the wagon and could have reached Leonard's door, but, discovering that his brother had not awakened, ran back to warn him and die with him.

With James Hanrahan were Bat Masterson, Billy Dixon, Mike Welch, Shepherd, Andy Johnson, Ogg, Watson, Clark and McKinstry — all but one, I believe, plainsmen, though young men.

With Fred Leonard were James Campbell, Edward Trevor, Frank Brown, Charley Armitage, "Dutch Henry," Billy Tyler, Old Sam Smith, Old Man Keeler, Fred Myers, and Fighting McCabe, who was Irish — some raw and some veterans.

Glancing from the windows, the men in Langton's found that the Indians had dismounted in the rear of their house and were giving a war dance in anticipation of an easy and immediate victory. A well-directed volley, however, soon dispelled this illusion, and the terpsichorean gentlemen resumed the more exacting duties of the day, which, as George Ebey very truly remarked, were "their best hold anyway."

The men at Leonard's were furnished with eight new Sharp's rifles, a case of which Leonard broke open and distributed.

Again and again the Indians dashed against the doors of the building in the endeavor to break them down; running at full speed, they hurled their horses against the defenses, or, whirling, backed them against the doors, hoping their weight would force an entrance. Long after the sun had risen in the heavens they continued to make frequent charges on the quarters of the hunters, retreating at intervals along the creek or behind the stockade.

The men at Hanrahan's completely covered the ground around Langton's except on his southern exposure; they had full control of the south of Leonard's stockade and nearly a clean sweep of Leonard's east side. Their adobe was the key to the situation; it probably saved Langton's small force and contributed materially to Leonard's defense.

The band which went after the hunters' horses found great difficulty, because, as Jim Hanrahan says, "no civilized horse will stand for an Indian;" sometimes they become restless when the red men are three or four miles away — there are no bathtubs among the Kiowas and Comanches. Hanrahan was firing at the Indians who were trying to steal the horses. He killed the pony of the man who was after his own big span — which the horse thieves found very troublesome — and having dismounted him thought he was about to get him.

Just then from the northwest came the sweet and welcome call of a bugle, which blew the rally and stirred the hearts of the hunters with the hope of rescue. Then came the shriller notes of the charge, the tramp of approaching horses, and from behind the stockade some fifty warriors precipitated themselves on Hanrahan's, at their head Stone Calf's nephew, his gallant conduct adding splendor to his magnificent apparel.

Fifty Indian bullets buried themselves in the adobe walls or tore through the windows. Three Winchester rifles and seven fifty-caliber buffalo-guns viciously replying, served notice that the white men knew their business and were fighting for their lives. During a long minute the pale specter struck the young men of the Comanches as swiftly as the Angel of Death smote the first-born of the Egyptians.

Straight at the window where was Hanrahan rode the young chief. The red man fired his pistol from a running horse and missed. The white man shot from a rest, quickly changing his aim from the distant horse thief to the unexpected apparition. Twenty feet the painted pony ran, rounding the north east corner of Hanrahan's adobe, before fled the spirit of the bravest young warrior of the

Comanche nation; Stone Calf's nephew, shot through the body by a fifty-caliber bullet, pitched from his pony, dead, within seven feet of the building whose mud walls he so boldly tried to storm. The long lance shivered when its point struck the ground and the dainty trappings quivered in the dust. As he went down his feather-covered streamers fluttered mockingly in the air, at last settling slowly about the form of the young warrior. His followers fell beside him or, fleeing from that terrific fire on fleet ponies, disappeared as quickly and as mysteriously as they came.

"Weep, you women in the wigwam! Mourn, you braves at the scalp dance! Never again shall Stone Calf's nephew ride to battle." Red Death rode the painted pony that day.

This charge was about the last direct attack upon Hanrahan's — the approaches were too poor and the marksmanship in that quarter altogether too good.

"Looks like we lost our popularity with them redskins the first dash out of the box," said Mike Welch.

At the northwest and southeast corners of the stockade were bastions. Leonard and Tyler went to the northwest one; but the Indians poked their guns through the port holes from the outside and fired. Leonard and Tyler retreated across the corral, firing as they walked. Pausing for a moment in the doorway to discharge one last volley, Tyler fell, shot through the lungs, and was quickly borne inside.

The hunters in the north building heard the Indians chopping up the Shadier wagon, and surmised they were about to fire the store. In all the houses, provisions had been utilized as barricades. Leonard, Armitage and "Dutch Henry" now quickly threw down the sacks of flour piled against the north side, punched out the chinking, and saw five Indians on their ponies by the wagon. Three rifles cracked, three Indians fell dead, and two decamped. A sixth, with a trumpet across his back and the Shadlers' canned stuff in his arms, sprang out of the wagon and ran north. This was the mysterious bugler, supposed to be a deserter from the regular colored cavalry, though Hanrahan and Dixon both have an idea that he was a half-breed raised by the tribe. Charley Armitage, a crack shot, promptly borrowed the forty-caliber rifle Leonard had had made for his own especial use, and — let Bat Masterson tell the story — "plunked a big forty- caliber bullet through him, and he bugled no more that day."

About sixty braves led by a young Kiowa chief dashed with fearless valor right at the big gate of Leonard's corral, just south of his building. So swift, so fierce was the charge, that the tramp of their horses rose like pony thunder in the ears of the men in Leonard's store. As they swept up to the barricade, the young Kiowa chief rapidly dismounted and attempted to throw open the gate to the corral. A dozen sharp shooters' rifles cracked. In the flash of an eye he was down and his pony gone.

Dismayed by his fall and the awful fire, after a few moments' desperate shooting at the windows, the ranks of the band were broken and they fled, unable to take away their chief or his fallen comrades. Wounded in three places, his hip bone broken, he lay for three hours in the June sun in view of all; then, evidently recognizing the impossibility of rescue or recovery, he drew a pistol, gave the war whoop of the Kiowas, shot himself through the head, and died. The young Kiowa and Comanche chiefs entered the Happy Hunting Ground side by side.

A better directed attack was now delivered against Langton's. Twenty braves dismounted and attempted to rush the door.

"If they had done this when they first came, we wouldn't have lasted a minute," says Jimmy.

But as it was, the Indians did not last a minute: the fire from Langton's and the cross-fire from Hanrahan's, where Dixon and Masterson had secured an advantageous

Bat Masterson

position, were too much for them, and after a desperate but futile conflict they fell back again. The first furious assault of the enemy was broken; in front of Leonard's and Hanrahan's, to the rear of Langton's and Hanrahan's, the ground was strewn with dead and wounded ponies and Indians, lying in the Texas sun. But the Indians returned to the charge, singly, in pairs, and in groups, eagerly, generally unavailingly, hoping to bear away their wounded and their dead.

But by this time excitement had given place to cool resolution and unerring precision of marksmanship. The Indians came on, waving their shields to deflect the bullets; but when a Sharp's rifle bullet hit a shield, "nothing was seen," says Bat, "but flying feathers and a dead Indian." Their efforts resulted only in additional fatalities. In one instance five of the red men fell across the chief they vainly sought to save, and the savages sullenly desisted.

James Langton

At Hanrahan's and Langton's, attention was now turned to the luck less braves, who, their ponies slain, had sought refuge behind the buffalo hides back of Langton's. The high grass half way from the hides to the hills was also full of them. "Those in the hills," says Hanrahan very justly, "showed traits of character that would be worthy of emulation by any race or color of men, exposing themselves freely to save their comrades." The men in the adobes could hear the Indians behind the buffalo hides engaged in continuous conversation with those in the high grass. The purpose was soon apparent: from the high grass came volley after volley at the windows so effectively that it was worth a man's life to appear there, even Masterson and Hanrahan being driven from the windows for the time. After a while, under cover of this fire, most of the Indians reached the high grass and were comparatively safe and well on their way to the hills, creeping on their hands and knees. Finally an Indian in the grass would give a peculiar whoop, a reply would come from the hills, and on the moment a couple of horsemen would emerge to his aid. Riding furiously, they would reach him as he rose to run, covering his escape and perhaps dragging him to a place of safety. They recklessly risked their own lives to succor their friends.

Billy Dixon and a sharp-shooter at Langton's combined on a feathered headdress which rose above a pile of hides some seventy-five yards from the store, a pony standing beside. For ten minutes the two hunters kept their savage foe dashing from corner to corner, unable to fix his exact location. The pony fell at the crack of Dixon's gun, and then Dixon sent a bullet right through the buffalo hides. The scorched quarry broke cover, giving short, sharp yelps like a coyote at every jump, and ran for the high grass. He has never drawn a government ration since.

Young Shepherd, discovering a dismounted red cavalryman behind a small sod outbuilding, took station above the window with his Winchester and began firing. At last he came down in disgust.

"Bat," said he, "I've fired at that cussed buck six times and missed him every time; you try it," and he boosted his friend to his place.

"Directly," says Masterson, "I saw Mr. Indian backing my way, getting out of range of fire from Bob Wright's store. I commenced getting a bead on him. As he backed an inch or two more I let fly and Mr. Indian bounded in the air about three feet, dropped his rifle and fell dead. I turned around to Shepherd and said, 'Shep, I got him the first crack.'"

"The Indians were very brave," says Jimmy Langton; "for hours they kept in range and died like men, and carried their dead and wounded off the field, all but thir teen dead." Yet by eleven o'clock in the morning they realized the futility of further effort to storm the hunters' quarters, and withdrew to the surrounding hills for long range firing. Langton, taking account of stock, found that all his canned goods had been shot off his shelves. Leonard availed himself of the opportunity to set up the cigars. Old Sam Smith suddenly discovered that in his eagerness to give their visitors a cordial welcome he had neglected to complete his toilet and had been fighting all the morning without trousers.

After this ineffectual attack and terrible loss the Indians were in a high state of excitement. They circled about the place, firing from under their horses' necks, dropping on their horses' sides and holding by their heels.

T.J. Leonard

A council of chiefs on a distant mound attracted the sharp-shooters' fire, and the Medicine Man's pony fell to the ground. As the Medicine Man had promised the war paint would render them invulnerable, he explained that the bullet had struck his pony where there was no paint. I believe Achilles's friends offered some similar explanation when he was found vulnerable, and even Fitzsimmons himself claims to have been drugged.

Taking umbrage at this uncalled-for attention, a young chief from the group fired on rode furiously toward Adobe Walls. He came within one hundred yards and circled off to the hills again, shaking his lance, waving his shield, and with much bravado challenging the hunters to come out and fight. His impotent wrath and his fiery sally aroused the amusement of the white men, brought a burst of derisive laughter, ironical cheers, and a shower of bullets, from which he escaped unhurt, riding off with loud-voiced defiance.

An even more desperately determined brave charged singly on Langton's. In admiration of his gallantry the chivalric Langton cried to the men to refrain from firing. The red knight rode rapidly to the window, fired his pistol at the border men, directly at George Ebey, and wheeled to retreat. Mr. Ebey thought this was carrying courtesy a little too far and retaliated by shooting the unlucky hero off his horse. Wounded to the death, without hope of rescue, lying at the door of his enemies, this plumed warrior of the prairies put his pistol to his head and closed an incident which would have ornamented the pages of Froissart's Chronicles.

About four in the afternoon a body of horsemen came from the hills northwest of Leonard's to make a charge, but being promptly received with a lively fusillade swerved into the hills again, though a few still lingered behind the buffalo hides, in the grass, in the willows, and more behind the stockade.

After the cessation of the fierce charges, the besieged in each building became anxious as to the fortune of their comrades. Bat Masterson, the youngest man at Adobe Walls, took the initiative, as he has in many adventures since. He suggested that he should go to Leonard's for some ammunition for Dixon's Sharp's rifle, and that Dixon and Hanrahan should go to Langton's. Hanrahan and Dixon made their way to the southern building, with some difficulty convinced the men within that they were not Indians, and climbed through the window to find all well. Dixon signalized his advent by killing an Indian at eight hundred yards, and remained, Hanrahan returning.

Dixon was a marksman not unworthy of Masterson's tribute: "Billy Dixon, who occupied half the window with me during much of the thickest of the fight, was a remarkable man, always cool, a dead shot no matter what the distance, never saying a word, always alert, looking for an opportunity to drop a bead on the enemy; and when he succeeded, whether Indian,

Indian pony or buffalo, whether standing, walking or running, Dixon always brought home the goods."

Masterson climbed through the window at Leonard's, found his friend Tyler dying, and with tender solicitude sought to ease and comfort his last hours. Not yet out of his teens, this young Jack Hamlin of the Southwest proved a careful and assiduous attendant. Gentle as a mother he raised the head of the dying lad, when Tyler called for water. There was not a drop left.

Out stepped Old Man Keeler, Leonard's cook, veteran plainsman, the oldest man there.

James Hanrahan

"Gimme the bucket."

Old Man Keeler sprang through the window which Young Man Masterson had entered a moment before. He walked straight across the corral to the pump by the mess house.

The Indians hidden behind the west of the stockade immediately opened fire. Keeler's dog ran out from its hiding place and crawled between his feet. The pump, whose every stroke they could hear, was an ancient and dilapidated affair. With each movement of its handle the rasping squeak could be heard half way to the hills and grated on the ears of the men in Leonard's store like the ticking of the fatal clock to a death watch. Volley after volley came from the west end of the stockade sixty yards away. They shot the dog to death between his master's feet. "A shower of bullets fell about him," says Masterson. But the old man pumped that bucket full for the dying boy within and turned back to the store window. The blaze from their guns was so fierce and constant, "it seemed," says Fred Leonard, "as if the whole west side of the stockade was on fire. They were all shooting at Keeler. There were twenty bullet holes in his dog."

But Old Man Keeler, cook, hostler, roustabout, hunter, frontiersman, warrior, prince, knight, gentle man and hero, walked leisurely across the corral, lifted the bucket up to the window and came in after it untouched. His boss says, "He didn't seem to think much of it."

But Keeler glanced back at his old and faithful friend. "I'd like," said he, "I'd like to git the devilish Injun that shot my dog."

King David's messengers who brought water from the well at the gate of Bethlehem never took half the chances Keeler took to carry a drink to the hunter boy on the Texas plains. Fame has missed him, but Glory and Honor stand sentinel over the buffalo grass that covers Old Man Keeler's lonely grave.

"I took some of the water, washed Tyler, bathed his face, and gave him a drink; then, with the roar of a hundred guns outside the stockade in his ears, his head fell over to one side, and Billy Tyler was dead," said William Bartley Masterson.

By five o'clock in the afternoon the enemy were driven from the shelter of the stockade to the hills. But the fighting continued at long range till sundown. The Indians claimed at the agency afterward that the white men used reflecting glasses or some fatal necromancy, for the Medicine Man was slain by a chance ball while behind the hills. Tradition alone preserves the memory of his deeds, his stratagems and his oratory.

When the firing ceased, Masterson and Frank Brown, Leonard's plucky clerk, went out, examined the Shadlers' wagon and reported their death, settling the hope that they might have escaped to the creek; and, when night fell, William Tyler, Isaac Shadier and his brother were buried in one grave, and there they have slept for thirty-three long years.

"Brick" Bond, coming in from the Palo Duro with a load of buffalo hides, heard the battle three miles away, unhitched his team and took to the brush till evening, when he slipped unmolested into Leonard's stockade. The next day two more hunters straggled in unnoted by the Indians. On this, the day after the fight, not a shot was fired.

The Indians were busy burying their dead and caring for their wounded, the white men in preparing for another battle. That night a number made their way through the Indian lines and scoured the prairie for miles, warning their straggling comrades.

On the second day Hanrahan's place was abandoned, and the force was divided equally between Leonard's and Langton's because of the large stock of goods to be protected there. Wells were dug and the places amply fortified.

That night a hunter named Reed went out of the camp and across the prairie toward Dodge City for reinforcements, for which he received the magnificent sum of a hundred and twenty-five dollars.

At sunrise on the third day the battle opened with brisk volley firing by the Indians from the willows at the base of the big butte on the east, by the creek. The buffalo hunters promptly replied, and the Indians were dislodged from that point. All day the Indians circled about the place in little groups and carried on the battle at long range, withdrawing behind the hills from time to time.

That afternoon William Olds of Warsaw, Missouri, was accidentally killed by his own gun on the roof of Langton's place during an Indian sally, and fell through the trap-door of the roof, dead, at the feet of his wife, the only white woman in all that country, except Quanah Parker's mother. The sons and daughters of Missouri have blazoned the way for the American people to every prairie ford and through every mountain valley, and this woman carried herself through the entire siege like a worthy daughter of the state from which she sprung.

By five o'clock in the morning of the following day over a hundred hunters had crowded into Adobe Walls from the surrounding territory, making their way in before the Indians were prepared for the contest. They kept on coming till very nearly all in the Texas Panhandle except those slain by the Indians had sought the city of refuge.

Two days of quiet followed, and it was thought the Indians had departed. Tobe Roberts and Huffman walked out to the sand hills for plums. Huffman was killed in sight of the Walls, but Roberts made his way safely back to the fortifications.

For a number of days they were surrounded and the firing continued, but finally the Indians withdrew, and on the morning of July 14th the hunters marched out for Dodge City, which they reached July 27th. A. C. Myers, Leonard's partner, had gone down with eighty wagons and brought away most of the stores, except six thousand buffalo hides. The Indians, who had lost eighty men killed and mortally wounded and two hundred ponies, burned the buildings, and only little mounds on what is now Sheriff William Dixon's ranch indicate the place where twenty-eight white men vanquished nine hundred Indians and began the campaign of 1874.

The hunter, Reed, who had gone for help, reached Dodge City with a letter from

Hanrahan to A. B. Webster, who telegraphed Governor Osborne of Kansas and the commanding officer at Fort Leavenworth. Osborne quickly forwarded a thousand stand of arms to Dodge City. The commandant at Fort Leavenworth, Hanrahan tells us, declined to believe that there had been any such contest, and declared that if there had been the hunters had no business to be there.

So the buffalo hunters and traders fought their own battle and made their own record, and the tale of Adobe Walls does not figure in those quaint romances known as the official reports.

The hunters who fought at Adobe Walls won renown from the Platte to the Rio Grande, but their deeds were never chronicled, their story was never told, and what were Achilles without a Homer?

Some day on the big butte over the valley will stand an Oklahoma granite statue of Old Man Keeler. One likes to think that as the moonlight falls on the Breaks of the Canadian, Time's kinetoscope unrolls its moving pictures and shows in dim review the sojourners in the valley, while some weird phonograph calls out the voices of the past! Across the Canadian file Aztec conquerors in cotton cuirass, swinging the somber banners of Montezuma and burning incense to Huitzilopochtli. An occasional Iroquois hunter spies out the land for those who would have been rulers of this continent but for the advent of the Anglo-Saxon. From the foot-hills of the mountains issue patient Pueblos of Taos and Acoma, returning stoop-shouldered with their winter meat. In their trail trot the steel-gleaming cohorts of the Spaniards, led by girdled friars, who raise the true cross and erect their adobe Mission, where soon the blue-stem grows over their altars. The Mexican hunter in big sombrero and gay serape rides swiftly across the scene. Vast herds of buffalo out of the north pause to graze the sweet grass and linger in the grove. Behind springs the painted savage, speeding swift arrow or casting keen lance. From the Arkansas come Bent, Bovient, French Canadian trappers with Kit Carson at their heels, to build the Adobe Walls, marry the squaws, trade with the Indians and disappear.

Printed in Great Britain
by Amazon